UNSPOKEN BATTLES

RISING ABOVE THE PAIN

Cornelius Garnett

Unspoken Battles by Cornelius Garnett

Published by Daniel Gomez Enterprises LLC / June 2026

Contact Info: (210) 663-5954 / Email: Info@DanielGomezGlobal.com

Paperback: ISBN: 978-1-97054-9 Hardcover: 978-1-970549-41-6

UNSPOKEN BATTLES

RISING ABOVE THE PAIN

Cornelius Garnett

DGE PUBLISHING

Daniel Gomez Enterprises, LLC

This book is dedicated to anyone who has ever felt alone.

TABLE OF CONTENTS

INTRODUCTION

Life has a way of shaping us long before we understand the forces at work. For some, childhood is a place of safety and belonging. For others, it becomes the first battlefield; quiet, unseen, and deeply formative. In *Unspoken Battles*, Cornelius Garnett invites readers into the hidden corners of his life, revealing the wounds, resilience, and hard-won wisdom forged through decades of adversity.

From the earliest pages, it becomes clear that Cornelius's story is not defined by a single moment, but by a series of experiences that left lasting marks. As he writes about his childhood in Kanata, Virginia, he describes a world where "*everyone you meet is fighting a battle you know nothing about.*" Those battles began early—bullying, instability, and the loneliness of feeling different in a place where conformity was the unspoken rule. The pain of those years was compounded by the chaos at home, where fear and uncertainty became daily companions.

Yet even in those early chapters, a quiet strength emerges. Cornelius survived not because life was gentle with him, but because something within him refused to break. Books, pets, and imagination became his refuge. Determination became his anchor. And hope—fragile, flickering, but persistent—carried him forward.

His journey into adulthood brought new landscapes but familiar struggles. The military offered escape, structure, and the promise of reinvention. Instead, it became another arena where he faced ridicule, isolation, and betrayal. "*I hadn't escaped anything; I'd just changed venues*," he reflects in one chapter, capturing the painful truth that unhealed wounds follow us wherever we go.

But this book is not simply a recounting of hardship. It is a testament to endurance. To growth. To the courage it takes to confront the past rather than run from it. Through therapy, self-reflection, and a willingness to face the darkest parts of his story, Cornelius begins the long process of healing—learning that strength is not the absence of pain, but the decision to rise despite it.

Unspoken Battles is more than a memoir. It is a mirror for anyone who has ever felt unseen, misunderstood, or alone. It is a reminder that trauma does not have the final word. And it is an invitation—to speak the truths we've buried, to acknowledge the wounds we carry, and to believe that healing is possible even after years of silence.

As you turn these pages, you will walk with Cornelius through the shadows of his past and into the light of his becoming. His story is raw, honest, and deeply human. But above all, it is hopeful. Because in telling his unspoken battles, he gives others permission to face their own.

CHAPTER 1

AN UNEXPECTED BEGINNING

Everyone you meet is fighting a battle you know nothing about be kind Always -Robin Williams

———†———

The morning air in Kanata had a distinct quality—heavy with humidity in summer, crisp and biting in winter—but it was always thick with something else, too: the weight of everybody knowing everybody else's business. In a town where a quick trip to Walmart meant running into at least three people who'd known you since birth, there was nowhere to hide. Not that I understood what I was hiding from back then. I was born in the late seventies to a mother who was barely more than a child herself, in a place where time seemed to move more slowly than the lazy Tahkwa River that gave our little marina town a purpose when tobacco was king. Kanata, Virginia, wasn't much" one through five to eight traffic lights, and you're through the town," as I'd later describe it to people who'd never heard of it, which was everyone. It was the kind of place where working-class folks lived, where farmers tended their land, and where most people had to drive to cities more than an hour away if they wanted to make real money.

My father, Vernon, was young, too scared and unprepared for the responsibility of raising a child. "I wasn't ready," I'd learn decades later when I finally confronted him. Instead of stepping up to support my mother who'd just graduated high school, he went off to college on a full-ride scholarship, leaving her alone with an infant.

My mother's older sister helped raise me until I was about four or five. We also lived with my maternal grandmother for a while. It wasn't ideal, but we managed. My paternal grandparents showed far more compassion and responsibility than their son. They were educators and well-respected in the community, and they gave me a sense of stability that I wouldn't appreciate until much later. In many ways, my grandfather filled the role of my absent father.

Around the time I was five, my life shifted again when my mother got married to a police officer. This man, Brutus, became my stepfather, and my mother soon had another son —my brother, who was five years younger than me. On the surface, things seemed to be improving. We moved into our own place, a regular family unit taking shape.

But beneath that veneer of normalcy, darkness was brewing. At first, Brutus was distant and unaffectionate. The arrival of a little brother isolated me even more. I craved attention and needed a father figure. Unfortunately, Brutus did start to notice me more and that was worse than being ignored. He rarely struck me but his language was abusive, cruel, and menacing.

"Why's this little turd always under foot?" "I'll give you something to cry about!" He was much worse to my mom—including physical abuse—especially when he was drinking, which became more and more frequent. He was an alcoholic, though I didn't understand what that meant at the time. What I did understand was fear—the kind that makes a child's stomach knot up when they hear a certain car pull into the driveway, an all-too-familiar pace of footsteps.

Brutus didn't just bring violence into our home; he altered

the trajectory of my mother's life. She had always been sweet and gentle. After Brutus introduced her to drinking, her life turned down a dark, winding, dangerous road.

You'd think a police officer would be disciplined, follow the law, and protect rather than harm. But Brutus wore a mask. Nobody really knew what happened behind our closed doors —not my aunts and uncles, not even my paternal grandparents, who remained involved in my life.

Then came the robberies—not at all what you'd expect from an officer of the law. These weren't carefully planned heists. He'd have a few drinks and go knock off a little grocer or a liquor store. Unsurprisingly, he was busted and put on a leave of absence from the department.

With no income coming in, our situation deteriorated quickly. Bills piled up. Cars were repossessed. Brutus hid the vehicles to avoid the repo men, but they found them anyway. The tension in our home reached a breaking point. Brutus dialed up his already excessive drinking.

One night—a night that would change everything—Brutus decided to rob another store. My mother tried to stop him. I remember her crying, pleading with him not to go. But he took a shotgun and stormed out.

The next morning, I heard the phone ring and then my mother wailing. I peeked into the room, scared that she was fighting off Brutus again, but she was alone, collapsed on the floor, sobbing.

Brutus had strolled into a convenience store where a sober and well-armed clerk had shot him when confronted with a shotgun. My stepfather was dead.

Just like that, my mother became a young widow, with two boys to raise on her own. I was about ten; my brother was five. Too young to fully comprehend death but old enough to feel its impact reverberating through our lives.

We moved again, back in with my grandmother, before eventually getting our own place. Through it all, my mother did her best to hold things together. Even though she was sometimes impaired, she always made sure that we had the basic necessities. She didn't drink every day, but Brutus' influence lingered like a ghost, pushing her toward the bottle when the pain became too much.

Meanwhile, I was trying to navigate the treacherous waters of elementary school. From the very beginning, I was marked as different. I don't know if I was initially targeted because I was quiet and shy or if I made the mistake of doing something odd. I could have worn a shirt backward or tripped on the playground; kids can cruelly turn the slightest misstep into a defining characteristic that makes the victim an outsider. Whatever initial social faux pas pushed me to the margins made all subsequent actions confirmation that I deserved the abuse I was getting and I was not equipped to change my unfortunate placement in this category with words or actions.

The taunting focused mainly on my appearance—I had long eyelashes that some thought made me look feminine—and anything else they could find. "Gay," "acts like a girl," "faggot," "nerd"—the words followed me through hallways and out to the playground. I didn't even understand what most of the words meant, but I could feel the intent: words were meant to hurt.

And it worked. I had no friends. Lunchtime became a daily exercise in humiliation, trying to find a place to sit where I wouldn't be mocked. Often, I would find a quiet child to sit near—not because we would talk, but so I wouldn't be so obviously alone.

My life wasn't without some comfort and solace. My trusted companions were the menagerie of pets in my home: cats, dogs, gerbils, hamsters, guinea pigs, turtles, frogs. They didn't judge me. They didn't call me names. They just offered unconditional love. I dreamed of becoming a veterinarian when I grew up, finding meaning in a life dedicated to caring for creatures who had been such a comfort to me.

My academic performance remained strong despite everything. Books became another escape, a place where I could disappear from the cruelty of my peers and the chaos at home. Teachers were generally kind, but they either didn't notice the bullying or didn't know how to stop it. And I never told my mother or grandparents what was happening. How could I? My mom was fighting her own demons, and my grandparents—successful educators with high expectations—wouldn't understand.

Bullying wasn't discussed in black culture. This wasn't like racism where I could forge solidarity with others of my race and resist the oppressors. Everyone was my oppressor and it had nothing to do with the color of my skin. I was alone.

The isolation grew unbearable. Around eighth or ninth grade, I did something that terrifies me to even recall: I wrote a suicide note to my mother. I didn't know that's what it was. All I knew was the feeling that consumed me was one I didn't want to carry anymore. I didn't use words like "bullying" or "depression" because I didn't know that's what was happening. I just wanted to end my pain and loneliness. The solution I was seeking should have been clear to any adult who read my rambling note.

My mother showed the paper to my aunt. My aunt asked if I was okay. I said yes, confused by their tepid response to my desperate cry for help. And that was it. Nothing changed. No therapy, no interventions, no heart-to-heart conversations. Just silence.

So, I did what I had been doing all along—I kept going. I kept my head down, kept doing my schoolwork, kept enduring the taunts and isolation, and kept pretending I was fine when I was breaking inside. I carried on through elementary school and into intermediate school, a dark cloud always hanging over me, invisible to everyone but crushing in its weight.

Years later, looking back on that scared, confused child, I would wonder how I survived at all. But I did, carrying these early wounds with me as I continued my journey—wounds that would shape me in ways I couldn't yet imagine, for better and for worse.

The puzzle pieces of my childhood didn't fit together neatly. They were jagged and mismatched, some pieces missing entirely. But they formed the foundation upon which everything else would be built—the pain, yes, but also the resilience that somehow kept me moving forward, one day at a time, into an uncertain future.

Unspoken Truth Reflections:

1. What part of my childhood story have I never fully acknowledged, even to myself? *(This could be fear, instability, bullying, loneliness, or something I witnessed but didn't understand at the time.)*

____

____

____

____

2. Where did I learn to hide my feelings or silence my needs? *(Was it at home? At school? Around certain people?)*

____

____

____

____

3. How have those unspoken childhood truths followed me into adulthood? *(In relationships, confidence, boundaries, self-worth?)*

____

____

____

____

"The Lord is close to the brokenhearted and saves those who are crushed in spirit." — Psalm 34:18

Unspoken Battles Journal:

CHAPTER 2

SURVIVING THE SOCIAL GAUNTLET

My grace is all you need for my power is the greatest when you are weak. -Corinthians 12:9

———†———

The transition to high school in 1993 loomed like an execution date. After years of torment in elementary and intermediate school, I couldn't imagine how things could possibly get worse—but somehow, I knew they would. Piedmont County High School meant eighth through twelfth grade all in one building, which translated to more potential bullies, more hallways to navigate, and more opportunities for humiliation.

My academic abilities had always been a double-edged sword. On one hand, good grades kept my educator grandparents satisfied and gave me a sense of accomplishment in a life otherwise devoid of victories. On the other hand, academic success branded me with the "nerd" label—another reason for the tormentors to target me. The pressure to maintain my grades while surviving the daily social gauntlet was crushing.

The school building itself seemed designed for my particular nightmare. The cavernous cafeteria with its unspoken social territories. The echoing locker rooms where there was nowhere to hide. The long hallways where a stray comment could follow you all day. I developed a sixth sense for danger, learning which routes to take between classes to minimize encounters, which bathroom stalls were safest, and which corners of the library offered the most protection.

In eighth grade, I still clung to my studies as a lifeline. My grades were superb, but the cost was my visibility. Every raised hand, every correct answer, every good grade posted on the board reinforced my outsider status. I had an unspoken agreement with myself: excel academically, survive socially, and count the days until freedom.

But in ninth grade, something broke inside me. The relentless pressure began taking its toll. My grades started slipping midway through the year. The very thing I had used to define myself—academic achievement—became another casualty of my silent war.

Marshall Luck emerged as the ringleader of my tormentors. He was on the track team, popular, and seemed to derive particular pleasure from making me his target. His influence was such that even kids who might not have bothered me on their own joined in when he started something. He would mock my walk, my voice, my clothes, anything to get a laugh at my expense.

"Look at James with his high waters!" they'd jeer when my pants were too short, a result of growth spurts and my mother's limited budget for new clothes.

One particularly cruel incident happened during a fire drill. We had to form up on the track field, and as I was walking alone (as usual), Trevor Cartwright—another frequent tormentor—pushed me to the ground for no reason. I fell hard, and everyone laughed. The humiliation of having to stand up, dust myself off, and continue walking as if nothing had happened still burns in my memory. How did I even get up and keep going? Looking back now, I don't know where I found the strength.

My grandparents, concerned about my slipping grades, pressured me to get involved in sports—to be more like my father and uncle who had been athletes. While my grandfather mostly kept his thoughts to himself while helping me with homework or arranging for a tutor, my grandmother had been particularly adamant that I needed extracurricular activities. "You need an outlet," she insisted, not understanding that throwing me into another social situation would only expand my battlefield.

I reluctantly joined the track team, partly to appease my family and partly in a desperate attempt to shed the "nerd" label. It was a miserable experience. Marshall was there, ensuring I never felt welcome. The coach didn't care much about my performance or lack thereof. I was inconsistent in showing up for practice, making lame excuses to avoid the additional torment. I tried cross-country too, thinking the white kids might be less cruel, but the results were the same—isolation, mockery, and a deepening sense that I simply didn't belong anywhere.

In a misguided attempt to fit in with the Black students who seemed to reject me, I deliberately sabotaged my academic performance. I stopped raising my hand in class. I skipped assignments. I talked back to teachers. I got in-school suspension. My grandparents were baffled by the change. They arranged tutors and meetings with teachers, but none of them thought to ask me what was really going on.

By tenth grade, my rebellion was in full swing. I barely passed my classes. My behavior at home deteriorated too—I was disrespectful to my mother, who was dealing with her own demons. I occasionally stayed with my grandparents to escape the dysfunction at home, but even there I couldn't find peace. My grandmother would come into my room in the mornings to "encourage" me before school, but her words felt like nagging to my teenage ears. She didn't understand that I was dreading another day of torment.

I began working at Walmart during eleventh grade, less for the money and more for the escape it provided. Every hour at work was an hour away from school and home. I saved what I could, knowing I would need resources to get away from Kanata as soon as possible.

Lunch periods were particularly nightmarish. I often skipped the cafeteria altogether, choosing instead to sit outside at the front of the school until the bell rang, signaling the next class—geography with Mr. Johnson. On the days I did brave the cafeteria, I'd find a corner spot and eat quickly, head down, trying to be invisible.

My uncle worked as a janitor at the school, and sometimes he'd see me sitting alone outside during lunch. He never approached me or asked if I was okay. I often wondered if he heard what the other kids said about me, if he knew what was happening. If he did, he never intervened.

There were brief, desperate attempts at friendship. I tried to connect with Aaron Kent a quiet boy who lived on my grandparents' street. I thought maybe we could be friends—he was smart and seemed to keep to himself too. When I got my driver's license in eleventh grade, I offered to drive him to school. He accepted once or twice, then made excuses. That potential connection withered like so many others.

The girls in my classes presented another complicated dynamic. Some showed interest in me, but often it was for the wrong reasons. They knew my grandparents had money, and a few tried to use me for that. I would sometimes steal money from my grandfather's wallet to give to these girls, desperate for any kind of positive attention. It was a terrible thing to do to my grandfather, who had always been good to me, but I was so hungry for acceptance that my moral compass faltered.

Even adults joined in the torment. Benny Archer, who worked at the high school and was considered a godson by my grandparents, would call me gay or feminine. His sister, a grown woman, would make similar comments. My safe haven at my grandparents' house was invaded by these adults who should have protected me but instead contributed to my pain. Somehow, amid all this, I managed to pull my grades up enough in eleventh and twelfth grade to graduate. I couldn't get out of there fast enough. There was no graduation party for me, no celebration. I simply went to my grandparents' house afterward, relieved that this chapter of my life was finally over.

College was the next step, though I wasn't particularly enthusiastic about it. My GPA had taken too much damage for me to get into a good four-year school, so I enrolled at Tahkwa Community College—just across the river, about twenty-five minutes from Kanata. It wasn't far enough away to escape completely, but it was a start.

At community college, I experienced something novel: academic success without severe social consequences. The campus was small, but the anonymity was refreshing. I didn't know everyone, and not everyone knew me. My grades improved dramatically—I was doing well again, enjoying learning for its own sake rather than as an escape.

But the respite wasn't complete. Some of my old high school classmates were on campus; I was mostly able to avoid them but not entirely. Warren Torgo, one of the white kids who had bullied me in high school, ended up at Tahkwa too. I overheard him telling another student about me, continuing the pattern of ridicule. It was a harsh reminder that even when I thought I was moving forward, the past had a way of catching up.

After two years at community college, I transferred to Christopher Newport University in Newport News. It was a mid-sized campus still undergoing construction and development. When I arrived, they were still building dorms, so I stayed in a hotel the university had purchased across from campus to house students.

The university experience should have been liberating, but by then, I was too damaged to fully embrace it. I was dating a girl, which helped keep the "gay" slurs at bay, but I still didn't know how to connect with people. I worked overnight shifts at 7-Eleven near campus, choosing again to isolate myself with work rather than engage socially. When I wasn't working or in class, I was sleeping through my classes, exhausted from overnight shifts and years of emotional battering.

As I entered my twenties, still struggling to find my place in the world, still carrying the scars of years of bullying and isolation, I felt lost and directionless. The wounds from high school hadn't healed—they had just scabbed over, ready to break open at the slightest touch. I had escaped Kanata physically, but mentally and emotionally, I was still that scared, lonely kid sitting by himself outside the school, waiting for the bell to ring.

I didn't know who I was or what I wanted. I only knew what I didn't want: to ever go back to that feeling of helplessness and rejection. I was biding my time, working jobs I didn't care about, taking classes that didn't inspire me, waiting for something to show me a path forward that led somewhere other than back to the pain I'd known for so long.

What I couldn't see then, what would only become clear with the perspective of years and distance, was that sometimes the way forward isn't a straight line. Sometimes it's a zigzag of false starts and stumbles. Sometimes you have to get completely lost before you can find your way. And sometimes, salvation comes from the most unexpected places—like a military recruiter on a college campus, offering an escape route I never would have chosen for myself.

Unspoken Truth Reflections:

1. What part of my high school experience still affects me today? *(This could be bullying, rejection, humiliation, or the pressure to fit in.)*

____

____

____

____

2. Where did I learn to shrink myself to survive socially? *(Was it in classrooms, hallways, the cafeteria, or around certain peers?)*

____

____

____

____

3. What silent battles was I fighting that no one around me ever noticed? (The loneliness, the fear, the exhaustion of pretending to be okay.)

____

____

____

____

"The Lord is my light and my salvation—whom shall, I fear? The Lord is the stronghold of my life—of whom shall I be afraid?" -Psalm 27:1

Unspoken Battles Journal:

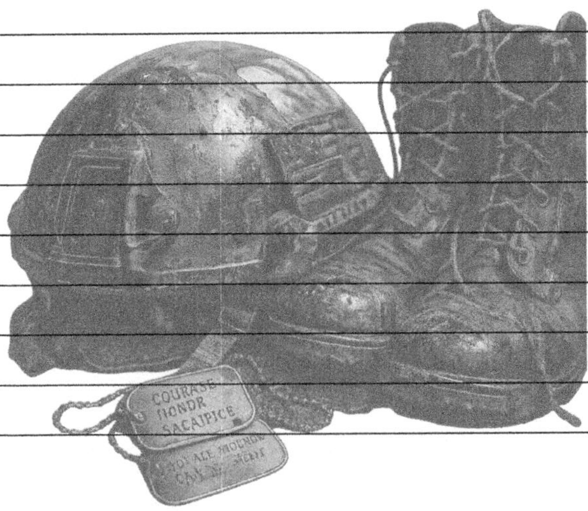

CHAPTER 3

A LEAP OF FAITH

Be strong and courageous. Do not be afraid, do not be discouraged for the lord your God will be with you wherever you go. -Joshua 1:9

———†———

My days at Christopher Newport University blurred together in a haze of sleep deprivation and obligation. I'd drag myself to classes during the day, work overnight shifts at 7-Eleven, then collapse in exhaustion only to repeat the cycle. The mid-sized campus was still under construction, much like my sense of self—incomplete, with essential parts missing. My grandparents were footing most of the bill, with Pell grants covering some expenses. I worked to contribute what I could, but more importantly, to avoid spending time in a social environment where I still felt like an outsider.

Academically, I was doing fine on paper. But I wasn't engaged. I was merely going through motions, turning in assignments, and trying to stay awake during lectures. My psychology and sociology classes should have helped me understand the very demons I was battling, but I couldn't make the connection. I couldn't see that I was studying exactly what I needed in my own life.

The university experience should have been transformative

—a chance to reinvent myself away from the small-town eyes that had watched and judged me for years. But freedom requires knowing what to do with it, and I had no idea. I carried my invisible scars from Kanata with me, a weight that kept me from moving forward even though I'd physically escaped.

One ordinary day in 2001 changed everything. I was crossing campus when a man in uniform approached me. An Army recruiter, sharp in his Class B uniform, looking more put together than anyone I'd seen in my directionless existence. The military had never once crossed my mind—not even as a passing thought. None of my family had served. My grandparents had pushed college as the only acceptable path forward. But something about this recruiter's confidence and the way he carried himself made me stop and listen.

He asked what I was doing at college, and I didn't have a good answer. When he described the structure, the training, the traveling opportunities, and most appealingly, the chance to reinvent myself completely, something clicked. Here was an escape route I'd never considered. Here was a path that would take me further from Kanata than I'd ever imagined going.

The recruiter suggested I take the ASVAB test to see if I qualified. I laughed it off at first—I wasn't interested in tests—but he persisted. When my scores came back, he seemed impressed. He talked about intelligence positions, security clearances, and bonus opportunities. I barely understood what he was describing, but I recognized an exit when I saw one. Everything happened with dizzying speed after that. Going to MEPS for the physical, choosing my MOS, signing papers—I moved through it all like someone sleepwalking, drawn forward by the promise of something different. I was completely naive about military life, but that didn't matter. All that mattered was that it wasn't here. It wasn't the life I'd been living.

Only after I'd signed the papers did I call my mother to tell her I was joining the Army. There was silence on the phone, then a quiet, "What?" I repeated myself, and her shock was palpable. My grandparents reacted similarly when I told them. They'd invested so much in my college education, and now I was abruptly changing course without consulting them. But what could they say? The papers were signed. The decision was made. My fate was sealed.

In truth, I wasn't joining to serve my country or out of some patriotic calling. I was running away. Running from Kanata, from memories of being bullied, from a sense that I didn't belong anywhere. I was chasing the possibility of becoming someone new—someone who hadn't been beaten down by years of isolation and ridicule.

In February 2001, I left for basic training at Fort Leonard Wood, Missouri. The winter landscape seemed fitting—barren and harsh, like the slate I hoped to wipe clean. I had no idea what I was getting into. I hadn't researched anything about the military. I didn't know about the regimens, the rules, the culture. I was walking in blind, armed only with desperation and the will to survive whatever came next.

Basic training hit like a tsunami from day one. The yelling drill sergeants, the rigid schedule, the constant demands for precision and conformity—it was a world away from the loose structure of college life. The physical demands were immediately apparent. Despite playing sports in high school, I wasn't in shape for the rigorous PT sessions. Push-ups, sit-ups, running—my body protested every new challenge. But failure wasn't an option. I'd come too far to wash out now.

What made basic training even more challenging was the social component. The Army's buddy system meant I was never alone—something that would have been a blessing in high school but felt like an invasion now. I'd grown accustomed to isolation. I'd learned to function as a solitary unit. Now, suddenly, my success depended on someone else, and theirs on me. If my battle buddy was late, I was late. If they failed, I failed. It was a crash course in interdependence for someone who'd never really trusted others.

Privacy became a luxury of the past. Sleeping in barracks with dozens of other recruits, showering in open stalls, using toilets with no doors—every aspect of military life seemed designed to strip away individual identity and rebuild us as a cohesive unit. For most, this was merely uncomfortable. For me, with my history of being targeted and ridiculed, it was terrifying.

The harassment I'd hoped to escape followed me to basic training. Different faces, same behaviors. "Hey, boo," they'd mock after I mentioned my mother's nickname for me during a rare moment of openness. The gay slurs, the comments about me "acting like a girl"—they were all too familiar. I hadn't escaped anything; I'd just changed venues.

But there was one crucial difference: in basic training, everyone was suffering. Everyone was being broken down. Everyone was struggling. In this shared misery, I found a strange sort of comfort. I wasn't being singled out for torment —it was a universal experience. And in that universality, I could disappear somewhat, blending into the collective struggle rather than standing out as a unique target.

Mental fortitude became everything. Don't show weakness. Don't break down. Don't give them another reason to single you out. I pushed through each day with gritted teeth and stubborn determination. The physical training got easier as my body adapted. The mental game never did.

Somehow, I made it through. I graduated basic training and moved on to Advanced Individual Training (AIT) in Pensacola, Florida, for my intelligence position. Six or seven months of technical training followed, but I still didn't really understand the world I'd entered. I was just going through the motions, checking boxes, surviving day by day.

My first duty station assignment came as a surprise: Germany. I'd never left the United States before. I'd barely left Virginia. Now I was being sent across the ocean to a country where I didn't speak the language, to work in a job I didn't fully comprehend, with people I didn't know or trust. The fear was overwhelming, but so was the relief of distance. An ocean between me and Kanata seemed like a good start.

Germany was beautiful in ways I couldn't appreciate at first. The fields, the architecture, the Autobahn with its dizzying speeds—it was all too much to process. I remember looking out the window as my unit picked me up from the airport, thinking, "What have I done?" For a brief moment, homesickness washed over me—not for Kanata, which I was glad to leave behind, but for my mother and grandparents, the few anchors in my turbulent life.

Military life overseas was supposed to create a sense of family among service members. That's what they promised in the recruitment materials—a brotherhood, a sisterhood, a bond forged in shared experience and mutual dependence. But old patterns reasserted themselves quickly. The bullying continued, now with the added element of homophobia in the hyper-masculine military environment.

I retreated into myself again, but with one significant difference: in Germany, I discovered alcohol. The country's beer culture made drinking not just accepted but expected. It became my coping mechanism, my way of numbing the loneliness and misery that followed me across the ocean. When I drank, the words hurt less. The isolation seemed less crushing. The mask I wore to navigate daily interactions felt less suffocating.

At twenty-two, I was learning destructive coping mechanisms that would haunt me for years. I was building a foundation for my adult life on the shaky ground of avoidance and self-medication. But in the moment, I saw no alternatives. I just knew that drinking helped, that it created a temporary buffer between me and a world that seemed determined to reject me.

My grandfather had been right about one thing: I had found an outlet. It just wasn't the healthy one he'd hoped for.

I was stationed in Germany from 2002 to 2004, and in those years, I became someone I didn't recognize—someone who drank to excess, who withdrew from genuine connections, who was just trying to survive each day without collapsing under the weight of accumulated traumas. The beautiful countryside, the historic cities, the cultural experiences—they were all backdrop to my internal struggle, barely registered through the fog of my pain.

So began a pattern that would persist through my military career and beyond—a pattern of geographic escapes without true healing. I changed locations like some people change clothes, always hoping the next place would be different, that the next assignment would be the one where I finally found peace. But the truth I wouldn't acknowledge for many years was simple and devastating: wherever you go, there you are. You can't outrun yourself. And until I learned who that self truly was—beyond the labels, beyond the trauma, beyond the masks I wore for protection—no amount of distance would ever be enough.

As I prepared for whatever came next in my military

journey, I still clung to the hope that somewhere, somehow, I would find a place where I could be myself—if only I could figure out who that was. The leap of faith I'd taken by joining the Army hadn't landed me in the safe haven I'd hoped for, but the journey was far from over. I was still falling, still searching for solid ground, still hoping that one day I would land somewhere that felt like home.

Unspoken Truth Reflections:

1. **What was I truly running from when I chose a new path?** *(Was it my past, my pain, my identity, or the fear of staying the same?)*

____

____

____

____

2. **What part of joining the military felt like my only escape?** *(Was it structure, distance, reinvention, or the hope of becoming someone new?)*

____

____

____

____

3. **What does the younger version of me need to hear about taking risks and starting over?** *(That he was brave, that he wasn't wrong for wanting more, or that healing often begins with a single step.)*

____

____

____

____

"See, I am doing a new thing! Now it springs up; do you not perceive it? I am making a way in the wilderness and streams in the wasteland."-Isaiah 43:19

Unspoken Battles Journal:

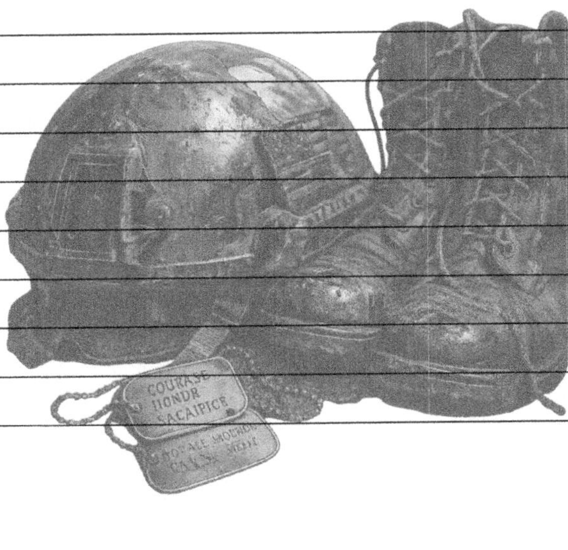

CHAPTER 4

DEMONS IN THE RISING SUN

———†———

I don't care if it hurts,

I want to have control

I want a perfect body

I want a perfect soul.

-Radio Head

———†———

When my transfer orders came through for an air base in Japan, I felt that familiar flutter of hope—the one that had carried me from Kanata to college, from college to the Army, and from the United States to Germany. Perhaps this time would be different. Perhaps this place would be the one where I could finally outrun my demons. I arrived in May 2005, stepping into a world unlike anything I had ever known.

Japan greeted me with a gentle beauty that was impossible to ignore, even through the fog of my personal struggles. Cherry blossoms painted the landscape in delicate pinks, and in the distance, the majestic silhouette of Mount Fuji stood sentinel over a land steeped in tradition and reverence. The base itself was small, but well-organized, nestled in the northern part of the main island where snowfall was plentiful in winter. Even the air felt different—crisp, clean, filled with possibilities.

I was assigned to a small detachment, no more than thirty soldiers, with the main unit stationed at a camp near a Japanese metropolitan center. Our work involved intelligence operations, the specifics guarded by security clearances and need-to-know protocols. The work itself was structured around shift rotations, providing a comforting rhythm to my days. I threw myself into my duties with an intensity born of necessity—when I was working, I wasn't thinking about everything else.

But as in Germany, the escape I sought remained elusive. The familiar pattern of isolation and torment followed me across the Pacific, taking on new forms but striking with the same precision. The military, with its heightened emphasis on masculinity and conformity, provided fertile ground for the same kind of bullying I'd endured throughout my life.

My past had taught me to be guarded, to keep my personal life hidden away from scrutiny. But in the claustrophobic confines of a small unit stationed overseas, privacy was a luxury I couldn't afford. Rumors and gossip traveled faster than official communications, and the smallest detail could become ammunition in the hands of those determined to make me an outcast.

It began innocuously enough. A chance meeting at the base PX led to a conversation with Braulio, a Puerto Rican service member. I didn't know he was in my unit when I first approached him, asking about household items as I set up my off-base accommodation. The realization came later—an awkward moment of recognition at a formation when our eyes met across the ranks. Something had sparked between us during that first meeting, a connection I hadn't expected but couldn't deny.

What followed was a complicated dance of secrecy and vulnerability. I was still trying to understand myself, still grappling with a sexuality I'd never fully acknowledged. I liked women—had dated them in high school and beyond—but I was also attracted to men. The word "bisexual" wasn't one I applied to myself then; labeling felt dangerous, like painting a target on my back that I'd spent years trying to remove.

Braulio and I began seeing each other, a relationship conducted largely behind closed doors. But while I craved discretion, bordering on invisibility, Braulio was different. He wasn't openly gay, but he wasn't hiding either. He had female friends who knew about us. He was comfortable with who he was in a way I couldn't comprehend, let alone emulate. To me, every shared glance, every moment spent together was a potential exposure, another chance for the world to

confirm what it had been telling me since childhood—that I was different, that I didn't belong.

My fears weren't unfounded. The whispers started soon enough. One night, after drinking with some unit members—something I did more frequently now, finding that alcohol smoothed the rough edges of my social anxiety—I mentioned that my mother had a nickname for me: "Boo." It was an innocent term of endearment, a mother's affection for her son. But in the hyper-masculine, often homophobic culture of the military, it became something else entirely.

The next day at formation, someone called out, "Hey, Boo!" followed by laughter that rippled through the ranks. In that moment, I was back in the elementary school cafeteria, the intermediate school hallway, the high school track field—exposed, mocked, reduced. What made it worse was that Braulio was there too, witnessing my humiliation but powerless to intervene without confirming the suspicions already swirling around us both.

Work became my only refuge, but even there, the harassment crept in. Comments about my mannerisms, my speech patterns, the way I carried myself—all delivered with a smirk and a sideways glance to ensure others caught the joke. Joseph, a soldier who claimed to see me as a brother, would call me "monkey" and beat his chest while making ape noises. It was juvenile, senseless cruelty, but it cut deep, nonetheless.

As the pressure mounted, I turned increasingly to alcohol. Japan's drinking culture, like Germany's, made this coping mechanism all too accessible. Every day after work, if I didn't have additional duties, I would head to the bar on base. The temporary relief of numbness became my most consistent relationship—more reliable than any human connection I'd formed.

This self-medication led to trouble. One night, I got into a bar fight with some Samoan service members—a hazy, alcohol-fueled confrontation that ended with damaged property and disciplinary action. I received an Article 15, a formal reprimand that included forfeiture of pay to cover the damages. It was a wake-up call, but not enough to break the pattern.

Meanwhile, my relationship with Braulio deteriorated into toxicity. We were both jealous and possessive, though his tendencies manifested more dramatically. The night he tried to run me over with his car outside a bar—all because he saw someone buy me a drink—should have been the final straw. I had stepped outside to talk to him, trying to diffuse his anger, when he accelerated toward me. I jumped back just in time, the screeching tires and bang of the vehicle stopping short still vivid in my memory.

Afterwards, full of rage and humiliation, I chased him to his house, pulled up the flowers from his yard, and tried to break in while he threatened me with a knife through the blinds. It was madness—two damaged people were extracting their pain from each other in the most destructive ways possible. Yet somehow, we continued this dance for months, trauma-bonded and isolated from healthier connections.

By 2006, I was struggling to maintain any semblance of mental health. The daily torment at work, the volatile relationship with Braulio, the increasing dependence on alcohol was all becoming too much to bear. I remembered when Sergeant Robinson in Germany had recognized the bullying for what it was, had told me not to let them get to me. But how do you not let something get to you when it's been the constant refrain of your entire life?

In the military, seeking help for mental health issues carried its own stigma. "Suck it up and drive on" wasn't just a saying; it was an ethos deeply embedded in the culture. Admitting weakness was anathema, particularly for someone already perceived as different. But after one particularly brutal day of harassment, when the weight seemed too heavy to carry alone, I made the decision to seek help.

The base had briefings on suicide prevention, with hotlines and resources available. I called one of those numbers and soon found myself sitting across from a behavioral health specialist. As I explained what was happening, the bullying, the relationship troubles, the drinking, I felt something shift. Here was someone who didn't laugh, who didn't dismiss my pain, who saw it for what it was: the accumulated trauma of years of rejection and isolation.

The specialist suggested medication and ongoing therapy, but I was resistant. I attended a few sessions, then stopped going. It felt too real, too exposed. Instead, I retreated back into my established coping mechanisms—work, alcohol, and the increasingly toxic relationship with Braulio.

When Braulio received orders to return to the States in 2007, our tumultuous relationship finally ended. He wanted to continue long-distance; I knew that would be a disaster. The separation was painful but necessary, leaving me even more isolated but perhaps slightly less volatile.

For three years, from 2005 to 2008, I served in Japan, living a life divided. On one side was the beauty of a country I could appreciate only in glimpses—the snow-covered landscapes, the respectful culture, the ancient temples juxtaposed against modern cities. On the other side was my internal landscape, increasingly barren and hostile, populated by demons I couldn't exorcise.

I didn't know it then, but Japan marked a turning point in my journey—not because it healed me, but because it brought me to the brink. It showed me the depths to which unaddressed trauma could drive a person. It revealed the limits of geographic escapes and the futility of trying to outrun oneself. It taught me that changing locations without changing patterns is like changing the frame on a painting while leaving the image untouched.

By the time I received orders for my next assignment in 2008, I was more fractured than when I'd arrived. The pieces of myself that I'd been trying to hold together were falling apart faster than I could gather them. Japan, with its contrasts of beauty and pain, had been both crucible and mirror—burning away my illusions while forcing me to see reflections I'd been avoiding for years.

As I packed my belongings, preparing for yet another move, yet another fresh start, I couldn't help but wonder if this pattern would ever break. If I would ever find a place where I could be whole, where the ghosts of Kanata and all the stations in between would finally release their hold on me. The rising sun of Japan was setting on this chapter of my life, but the demons it had illuminated would follow me into the darkness, waiting for the next dawn to cast their shadows once again.

Unspoken Truth Reflections:

1. **What past wound still rises to the surface when I least expect it?** *(A memory, a fear, a voice, or a moment that still has power over me.)*

____

____

____

____

2. **Which "demons" from my past do I still avoid confronting?** *(Old trauma, shame, anger, rejection, or unresolved pain.)*

____

____

____

____

3. **What truth about my past have I been too afraid to acknowledge?**
(Something I witnessed, endured, believed, or internalized.)

____

____

____

____

"The Lord is close to the brokenhearted and saves those who are crushed in spirit." — Psalm 34:18

Unspoken Battles Journal:

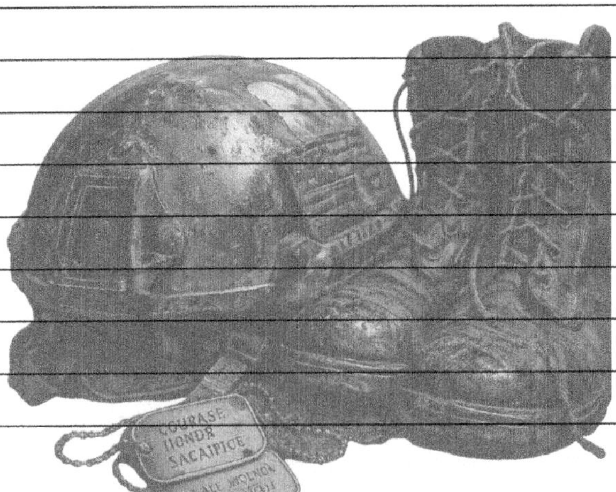

CHAPTER 5

TROUBLE IN THE LONE STAR STATE

My flesh and my heart may fail, but God is the strength of my heart and my portion forever. -Psalms 73:26

———†———

My station in Texas greeted me in 2013 with oppressive heat and another chance at reinvention. After fourteen years of service, I'd climbed to E-6, with soldiers under my command and responsibilities that should have given me a sense of accomplishment. Instead, I remained hollow, desperately seeking validation I never found.

The base was a machine that never stopped. Training for our Afghanistan deployment consumed every waking moment, a relentless pace I initially welcomed. The constant activity left no time to confront the darkness I'd carried from Japan to Georgia and now to Texas. I threw myself into preparing my soldiers, focusing outward instead of inward.

Just before deployment, everything changed. Command reshuffled personnel, placing me with an entirely new team—people who didn't know me and, more importantly, didn't seem to want to. My new first sergeant, Devlin, took an immediate dislike to me for reasons I couldn't understand. What I would discover later was that he'd been questioning others about me from day one, gathering ammunition for what was to come.

We deployed in late 2013 for what would become a ten-month tour of personal hell. Our unit provided intelligence support as bases closed during the drawdown. My team operated from a small forward operating base, conducting operations critical to force protection. From the beginning, the missions felt disjointed, the guidance insufficient, the setup designed for failure.

One particular mission epitomized everything wrong with the situation. I received orders to accompany a team outside the wire with minimal preparation, unfamiliar equipment, and a vehicle I barely knew how to operate. When I admitted my inexperience with certain systems, Nance and Shank—fellow soldiers I mistakenly trusted—took detailed notes on every perceived mistake, every hesitation. These notes would later become sworn statements against me.

Each day became a struggle to survive, not just the dangers of Afghanistan but the psychological warfare waged by my own leadership. The toxic racism permeating military culture reached new heights in this isolated environment. As a Black NCO, I noticed the difference in treatment, the way Devlin questioned others about my competence, the subtle and not-so-subtle undermining of my authority.

The betrayal culminated in August 2014. Called into a room with the command team, I was blindsided with an Article 15 for dereliction of duty. The allegations claimed I had fallen asleep on mission, that I didn't know critical equipment, that I was incompetent and a liability. In reality, I had been set up from the start, sent out without proper training, then punished for the inevitable result.

The truth didn't matter—the decision had been made before I even entered the room.

The punishment was swift: reduction in rank to E-5, forty-five days of extra duty, and forfeiture of pay. Fifteen years of service counted for nothing. The only small mercy was that they didn't revoke my security clearance—"because you're a good soldier," the lieutenant colonel said, a statement so contradictory it bordered on absurd.

After the Article 15, I remained in Afghanistan, stripped of rank and dignity, forced to work alongside those who had orchestrated my downfall. I went to mental health every day, harboring dark thoughts toward those whose betrayal cut deepest. Only therapy appointments and medication kept me from acting on these impulses.

I tried filing an Equal Opportunity complaint, hoping someone would recognize the racial component of what had happened. The EO representative agreed to meet but never showed up. She couldn't even look me in the eye afterward—another person choosing the path of least resistance rather than challenging toxic leadership.

Returning to Texas in late 2014, I fought to be moved away from the unit that had betrayed me. Eventually transferred to brigade, I found leaders genuinely puzzled by what had happened. They gave me responsibilities and treated me with respect, highlighting by contrast the injustice I had suffered. But it was too late—the damage was done. I spiraled into self-destruction. Alcohol flowed freely, and sex became another escape—meaningless encounters with men and women alike, seeking connections that remained elusive. These poor bandages couldn't cover the gaping wounds of betrayal and loss.

By 2015, I knew my active duty career was ending. With the demotion, I would hit service limits for my rank. The Army was downsizing, pushing out soldiers with black marks on their records. I could have fought the Article 15, appealed, tried to get my rank back—but the fight had left me.

Looking in the mirror, I barely recognized myself. Where was the hopeful young man who had joined to escape his past? Where was the dedicated NCO who mentored young soldiers? I had no answer. I didn't know who I was anymore.

I decided to transition to the Reserves rather than leave entirely, unable to completely discard fifteen years of service. But sitting in that barracks room, a thousand miles from anywhere I'd called home, I finally understood a truth I'd been running from: no matter where I went, what uniform I wore, or what rank I held, I couldn't escape myself. The pain woven into my being since Kanata would follow me until I found the courage to face it directly.

As 2015 unfolded and my time in Texas ended, I stood at another crossroads—one of many in a life defined by departures. But this time was different. I understood that my next journey couldn't be measured in miles or marked on any map. It would be a journey inward, through territories more frightening than any battlefield I'd encountered, with no guarantee I possessed the courage to take that first step.

Unspoken Truth Reflections:

1. **What part of this season revealed wounds I thought I had already healed from?** *(Old triggers, buried emotions, or patterns I didn't realize were still active.)*

2. **Where did I feel the most out of control during this chapter of my life?** *(Emotionally, financially, mentally, or in relationships.)*

3. **Which relationships in this season exposed deeper issues within myself?** *(Trust, boundaries, self-worth, or unresolved trauma.)*

____

____

____

____

My flesh and my heart may fail, but God is the strength of my heart and my portion forever. -Psalms 73:26

Unspoken Battles Journal:

CHAPTER 6

—†—

I will instruct you and teach you the way you should go;

I will counsel you with my loving eye on you.

—Psalm 32:8

Stepping out of the uniform that had defined me for fifteen years felt like having my skin peeled away. In 2015, I exited active duty not with the triumphant retirement ceremony I'd once envisioned, but as a broken man searching for scraps of identity among the ruins.

Those first civilian days were disorienting. The military, for all its flaws, provided structure. Now, I woke without a formation to attend, without subordinates looking to me for guidance, without the weight of a uniform that told the world who I was. The question I'd avoided for decades loomed large: Who was Caesar James without all the external markers?

The job hunt became my first taste of civilian reality. Interview skills weren't part of basic training. I bounced between odd jobs, each feeling more disconnected from my training than the last. My sexuality remained a confusing, painful subject. As a Black man trying to navigate bisexuality, I felt caught between communities, belonging nowhere.

Unwilling to completely sever military ties, I joined the Army Reserves in 2015. It seemed like a compromise—maintaining some connection to the structure I knew while building a civilian life. But my depression intensified. My therapist regularly submitted notes to my detachment, excusing me from monthly maneuvers when my mental health deteriorated.

The reserve unit leadership offered little support. The same pattern of slurs and mind games that had poisoned my active duty service followed me. The brotherhood that should have defined military service remained elusive.

In desperation, I considered returning to active duty—a step my therapist strongly advised against. I sought training in IT, hoping for direction, but still felt like an outsider everywhere. My old coping mechanisms—alcohol and meaningless sexual encounters returned with a vengeance. After a drunk and disorderly charge in 2017, I was forced into Alcoholics Anonymous, confronting yet another system where I didn't belong.

My reserves experience deteriorated until I requested inactive status. The approval came through, but being completely untethered proved frightening rather than liberating. I returned to active reserves, only to be medically retired in 2020. The chapter that began with such hope in 2001 ended with paperwork and processing out.

Throughout these years, I played endless rounds of the "what if" game. What if I'd never joined? What if I'd fought the Article 15? The questions circled like vultures, finding no answers but leaving deeper wounds with each pass.

Desperate for purpose, I accepted an overseas contracting job—returning to Afghanistan, the very place that had broken me. The irony wasn't lost on me, but the salary was substantial. It was meant to be a six-month contract, but I returned after only three, unable to bear the flashbacks and anxiety the familiar landscape triggered.

at each new destination. Panic attacks ambushed me in grocery stores when someone's tone echoed a former commander's. Trust became theoretical rather than emotional—something I understood intellectually but couldn't embody.

Loneliness became my constant companion. Even in crowded rooms, I felt fundamentally separate. I dated occasionally but kept partners at arm's length, afraid to reveal too much, unsure what "myself" even meant.

My drinking escalated dangerously. Blackouts punctuated my weeks with frightening blank spaces. I engaged in increasingly risky behaviors, testing whether anything could still make me feel something genuine. The spiral was obvious even to me, but stopping it seemed impossible.

One brutal morning in 2021, after a night lost to alcohol and regrettable decisions, I found myself staring in the bathroom mirror. My mother had passed away recently, another profound loss. The face looking back was unrecognizable—bloated from drinking, eyes dull with despair, a stranger wearing the mask of a middle-aged man who hadn't truly lived. Something shifted that morning. I mustered the courage to walk into a VA center and ask for help—real help. I sat across from a counselor and, perhaps for the first time, held nothing back. I spoke about the bullying in Kanata, the betrayal in Afghanistan, my sexuality confusion, the alcohol, the isolation, all of it.

The counselor outlined a treatment plan that seemed both impossibly demanding and absolutely necessary. Intensive therapy. Medication management. Support groups for veterans, addiction, and trauma. It would require vulnerability I'd spent a lifetime avoiding. I began unpacking my baggage piece by piece. Confronting my sexuality meant acknowledging the hurt by years of slurs. Processing military trauma meant accepting that I'd given my best years to an institution that failed to protect me. Addressing alcohol abuse meant finding healthier ways to cope with emotions I'd been drowning for decades.

The road wasn't straight, and progress wasn't linear. There were relapses, setbacks, days when getting out of bed required heroic effort. But slowly, things began to change. I developed tools for managing anxiety and anger. I explored my identity without the crushing weight of others' expectations. I began distinguishing between imposed labels and the truth of who I was beneath them.

Most importantly, I started getting to know and eventually love myself authentically. What did Caesar like? What brought me joy? What values did I hold that weren't imposed by family, military, or society? These simple questions required archaeological excavation of layers of conditioning and trauma. The healing journey isn't a destination you reach and declare complete. It's ongoing, demanding constant attention, like tending a garden always at risk from drought or storm. But for the first time since I was that frightened child in Kanata, I felt I was moving in the right direction—not running from pain, but walking toward understanding.

As I approached my mid-forties, I carried scars from all I'd been through—visible in facial lines, occasional nightmares, and vigilance that never disappeared. But I also carried something new: tentative hope that my life's second half might be lived with an authenticity and peace the first half lacked.

The military chapter had ended, but the broader narrative continued. There was unfinished business: relationships to heal, purposes to discover, wounds still tender to the touch.

eyes and an open heart—the bravest act of all for someone who had spent a lifetime in flight.

Unspoken Truth Reflections:

1. **What unresolved pain from my past still demands my attention today?** *(A memory, a relationship, a mistake, or a wound I never fully healed.)*

____

____

____

____

2. **Where do I still feel the weight of things I never dealt with?** *(Conversations left unsaid, emotions buried, or truths avoided.)*

____

____

____

____

3. **Which part of my story still feels unfinished or unresolved?** (A chapter I never closed, a person I never forgave, or a version of *myself I never healed.)*

I will instruct you and teach you the way you should go;

I will counsel you with my loving eye on you.

—Psalm 32:8

Unspoken Battles Journal

CHAPTER 7

BECOMING WHOLE AGAIN

Know that with God, all things are possible. -Matthew 19:26

—†—

The morning sun filtered through my townhouse windows as I sat cross-legged on the floor, eyes closed, counting breaths—in for four counts, hold for seven, out for eight. This simple technique, once dismissed as too basic for my complex trauma, had become an essential anchor in my healing journey.

After that pivotal day at the VA center, I approached therapy with the same determination I once gave my military career. In the Army, I'd pushed my body beyond limits to prove my worth. Now, I pushed my mind into uncomfortable territories, excavating buried pain with the understanding that exposure was the only path to healing.

Those early sessions revealed decades of repressed trauma —the bullying in Kanata, the betrayal in Afghanistan, the constant othering in every community I'd tried to join. The pattern emerged with painful clarity: I'd spent my life running from one place to another, hoping the next location would bring peace, only to find my demons waiting at each destination.

Mindfulness became my foundation—staying present rather than dwelling in the past or anxiously anticipating the future. My mind had been conditioned to constantly scan for threats, to replay past humiliations, to remain vigilant. Learning to bring my attention back to the present moment was like redirecting a river that had carved its course through stone over decades.

The breathing exercises grounded me when panic struck. The structured rhythm would gradually slow my racing heart, quiet the flood of stress hormones, and bring me back to the present. When a stranger's laugh reminded me of high school tormentors or when a particular tone of voice echoed military superiors, these techniques became lifelines.

My therapist introduced "opposite action"—doing the healthy things even when instincts screamed otherwise. When shame drove me toward isolation, I forced myself to reach out. When memories of betrayal stoked rage, I practiced forgiveness exercises. When self-loathing whispered I was unworthy of care, I deliberately engaged in self-compassion.

Group therapy provided unprecedented relief in discovering I wasn't alone. Others had experienced systematic bullying, crushing depression, and identity confusion. They too struggled with alcohol as self-medication and trust issues that made intimacy seem impossible. For the first time, I could speak about my sexuality without fear of judgment, exploring the complexity of being a bisexual Black man in environments with little tolerance for difference.

Journaling transformed nebulous thoughts into concrete words I could examine objectively. I kept a separate log of cognitive distortions, documenting when my thoughts veered into catastrophizing or black-and-white thinking. Seeing these patterns helped me challenge them, gradually retraining my brain to consider alternative interpretations.

Nature emerged as an unexpected sanctuary. On weekends, I would hike nearby trails, losing myself in the rhythm of boots against earth, the symphony of birdsong, the play of sunlight through the canopy. These experiences grounded me in a reality larger than my personal pain, reminding me that the world contained beauty alongside suffering.

I began volunteering at a local animal shelter, remembering how childhood pets had been such comfort when human connections failed. A three-legged cat named Widget particularly captured my heart. Despite his history of abuse, he approached each day with dignified resilience. I eventually adopted him and another cat named Carina, creating a small family built on unconditional acceptance.

Progress wasn't linear. There were days when old habits reasserted themselves, when accumulated trauma seemed too heavy to bear. The difference now was that I recognized these moments as temporary setbacks rather than fundamental failures. I had developed self-compassion—extending to myself the same understanding I would offer others with similar struggles.

When my mother passed in 2023, grief threatened to derail my recovery. In my earlier life, such loss might have sent me spiraling back into destructive patterns. Instead, I leaned into the tools I'd developed—allowing myself to experience the pain fully rather than numbing it with substances or distractions.

Her passing prompted me to reach out to my father, Vernon. Despite our minimal relationship throughout my life, I felt compelled to have an honest conversation. Our interaction was awkward at first but gradually opened into something resembling genuine communication. He admitted being scared and unprepared for fatherhood. Though this wasn't new information, hearing him acknowledge it directly brought unexpected peace. We ended with a handshake that evolved into a hug—not a fairy-tale reconciliation, but a step toward mutual recognition.

By mid-2023, I had assembled a toolkit for managing my mental health: meditation to quiet the mind, breathing exercises to regulate the nervous system, journaling to process thoughts, nature to provide perspective, therapy to guide healing, connection to combat isolation, and mindfulness to remain present. These practices weren't cures—decades-old wounds don't simply vanish—but they transformed overwhelming pain into something I could acknowledge and gradually integrate.

My current work in employee assistance services took on deeper meaning. Each time I connected an agency employee with mental health resources, I recognized the courage it took to ask for help. Though I kept my own struggles private professionally, my empathy came from intimate knowledge of both suffering and healing.

As I approached my mid-forties, I was still evolving—but for the first time, doing so authentically, without the masks that had once seemed essential to survival. I no longer viewed vulnerability as weakness but recognized it as the foundation of genuine strength and connection.

The work of becoming whole isn't completed in a chapter or even a lifetime. It's ongoing, requiring consistent attention and care. But there's profound difference between the exhausting vigilance of protecting wounds and the nurturing vigilance of tending to growth. One depletes; the other sustains. I think often of that frightened boy in Kanata who wrote a cry for help that went unanswered. I wish I could tell him that one day, he would find the courage to stop running, to turn and face what pursued him, to discover that healing began not with escape but with presence. I can't change his journey —my journey—but I can honor it by continuing forward with compassion for both who I was and who I am becoming.

The morning light shifts, casting new patterns across the floor. Carina stretches in her sunbeam, embodying perfect contentment in the present moment. Widget watches with knowing eyes that seem to see through all pretense. I take another breath—in for four, hold for seven, out for eight—and feel gratitude for this quiet moment of being simply, authentically myself.

Unspoken Truth Reflections:

1. What part of my childhood story have I never fully acknowledged, even to myself? *(This could be fear, instability, bullying, loneliness, or something I witnessed but didn't understand at the time.)*

2. Where did I learn to hide my feelings or silence my needs? *(Was it at home? At school? Around certain people?)*

3. How have those unspoken childhood truths followed me into adulthood? *(In relationships, confidence, boundaries, self-worth?)*

___

___

___

___

Know that with God, all things are possible. -Matthew 19:26

Unspoken Battles Journal:

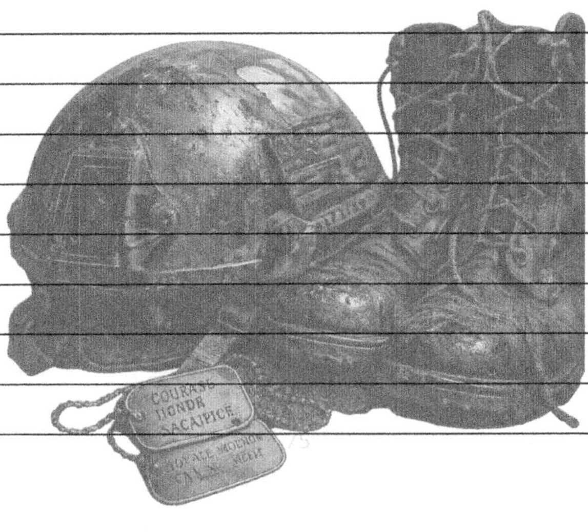

CHAPTER 8

MAKING PEACE WITH THE PAST

Do not grieve, for the Joy of the Lord is your strength. -Nehemiah 8:10

—†—

The autumn wind scattered golden leaves across my mother's grave as I stood there, wildflowers clutched in my hand. October 2023 marked the first anniversary of her passing, a loss that had temporarily derailed my recovery journey. For a brief, dark moment, the bottle had beckoned again with its false promises of comfort.

My relationship with my mother had been complicated. During my childhood, when bullying was at its worst, I'd perceived her as unavailable, too consumed by her own struggles to see mine. What I couldn't understand then was that she had been fighting her own demons—products of trauma I only partially understood.

In the years before her death, something shifted between us. As I began healing, I developed a different perspective on her life. She wasn't just my mother who had failed to notice my pain; she was a woman who had lost her husband to violence, raised two sons alone, and battled addiction without the resources to name what she was experiencing. We had learned, almost too late, how to be ourselves with each other.

The masks came off gradually, allowing us to see each other as two flawed, struggling humans who shared both blood and battle scars. She became my rock, my best friend. The irony wasn't lost on me—just as I discovered how to have an authentic relationship with her, she was taken from me.

Grieving her properly meant confronting other unresolved relationships, particularly with my father. Vernon had been a shadow presence throughout my childhood—physically close enough to visit but emotionally distant as a stranger. His absence had marked my psyche more profoundly than I'd acknowledged. How much of my desperate need for approval, my fear of rejection, my struggle to trust, traced back to that fundamental abandonment?

The question drove me to his doorstep—my grandparents' house, where he now lived alone in the basement. I knocked without warning, my heart hammering against my ribs. When he opened the door, shock registered on his face.

Our conversation was halting, awkward, freighted with decades of unspoken words. I told him how his absence had affected me, how I'd spent years wondering why I wasn't enough to make him stay. I wasn't accusatory; therapy had drained those emotions of their potency. I was simply honest in a way I'd never allowed myself to be with him before.

To my surprise, he listened and responded with his own honesty—admitting fear, unpreparedness, immaturity. He didn't make excuses or rewrite history. He simply acknowledged that he had been scared, that he hadn't known how to be a father. Nothing he said erased the past, but his acknowledgment was a balm I hadn't known I needed. Together, we shared memories of my mother, a bittersweet reunion forged in shared loss. The conversation didn't. transform us into the father and son we might have been, but it created space for a different kind of relationship—tentative, fragile, but honest.

As I left, we shook hands, and that handshake evolved into an awkward hug. I drove away feeling lighter, having set down a burden I'd carried so long I'd forgotten its weight. Forgiveness wasn't about excusing the hurt, but about releasing the stranglehold that resentment had on my life.

This process of making peace extended beyond the family. In therapy, I examined the other painful chapters of my story—the bullying in Tappahannock, the betrayal in Afghanistan. My therapist posed a question that stopped me: Did their motivations actually matter?

It was revolutionary. I had spent decades trying to decipher why classmates targeted me, why military superiors undermined me. As if understanding the "why" would make the pain more bearable. But the truth was simpler: nothing justified the pain they inflicted. Their actions reflected their limitations, not mine.

Gradually, I began viewing my tormentors with something approaching pity. They had missed the opportunity to know the real me, to share in the resilience and growth that emerged from the pain. Their loss was greater than mine.

This perspective shift came in fits and starts. One powerful exercise involved writing letters to myself at various ages—to the confused child in elementary school, to the isolated teenager, to the desperate young man joining the military, to the broken soldier returning from Afghanistan.

In these letters, I extended the empathy I had never received. I told young Caesar he was worthy, loved, and stronger than he knew. I assured teenage Caesar that the bullies' words reflected their insecurities, not his truth. I reminded military Caesar that his value wasn't determined by toxic leaders.

Reading these letters aloud in therapy often reduced me to tears—not just for the pain endured, but for the unnecessary shame carried for so long. With my therapist's help, I reframed the distorted narratives about my worth, separated others' cruelty from my own nature, and acknowledged the strength it took to seek help when the burden became too heavy.

I grieved for years, lost to self-loathing and destructive coping mechanisms. But my therapist encouraged compassion rather than regret. I had done the best I could with the tools available. Even my most self-destructive behaviors had been attempts, however misguided, to survive unbearable pain.

Perhaps the most profound shift came in releasing the need for external validation. From childhood through my military career, I had measured my worth through others' approval. Now, I was cultivating a sense of self untethered to any institution or relationship.

Making peace with the past wasn't a single event but an ongoing practice. Some days the old wounds felt fresh; other days I could look back with genuine compassion for everyone involved, including myself. The difference was that I no longer allowed those wounds to define me or determine my future. They were part of my story, but not the whole story.

One evening, sorting through old photographs, I found a picture from high school. There I was, awkward and uncomfortable, wearing a forced smile that didn't reach my eyes. Looking at that young face with all the knowledge I'd acquired since, I felt tenderness. That boy had no idea what lay ahead—the pain, yes, but also the growth, the discovery, the eventual path toward wholeness.

I placed the photo in a frame rather than back in its dusty box. Not as a reminder of pain, but a testament to the journey to acknowledge how far I'd come and honor the resilience that had brought me here. That boy deserved to be seen, not hidden away.

Making peace didn't mean erasing the past or pretending the hurt never happened. It meant integrating those experiences into a larger narrative—one where pain was not the conclusion but merely a chapter in a longer, richer story still being written. The autumn wind rattled my windows as evening fell.
Widget limped over, his three-legged gait a reminder that wounds can heal, that adaptation is possible, that life continues even after profound loss. Carina watched from her perch, eyes half-closed in contentment.

In this quiet moment, surrounded by the small family I had created, I felt something that had eluded me for most of my life—a sense of being exactly where I belonged, not running toward or away from anything, but simply present. The past still existed, with all its complexity. But it no longer stood between me and the possibility of peace. It had become, finally, just that—the past, not a prison.

Unspoken Truth Reflections:

1. What part of my childhood story have I never fully acknowledged, even to myself? *(This could be fear, instability, bullying, loneliness, or something I witnessed but didn't understand at the time.)*

2. Where did I learn to hide my feelings or silence my needs? *(Was it at home? At school? Around certain people?)*

3. How have those unspoken childhood truths followed me into adulthood? *(In relationships, confidence, boundaries, self-worth?)*

____

____

____

____

Do not grieve, for the Joy of the Lord is

your strength. -Nehemiah 8:10

Unspoken Battles Journal:

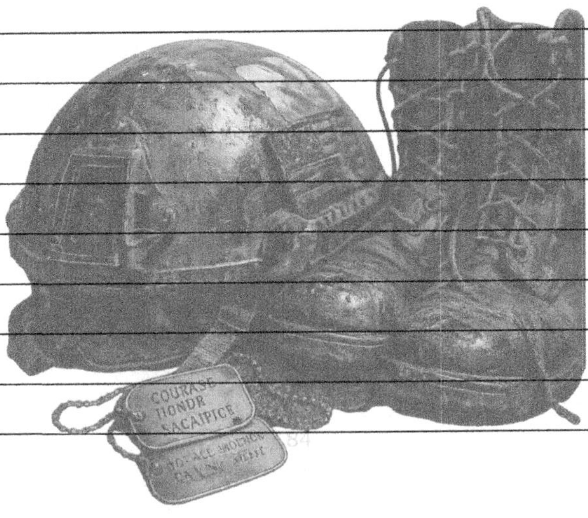

CHAPTER 9

EMBRACING AUTHENTICITY

Trust in the Lord with your heart and lean not on your own understanding; in all your ways submit to him.

-Proverbs 3:5-6

—†—

The early morning sun cast gentle light through my living room window, illuminating dust particles that danced in the air like tiny constellations. I sat at my desk, fingers hovering over the keyboard, preparing to write the most difficult chapter of my life—not this memoir, but the authentic life I was finally ready to claim. For decades, I had existed in fragments, compartmentalizing different aspects of my identity to survive environments that demanded conformity. Now, I was undertaking the painstaking work of integration, of becoming whole.

My sexuality had been a source of confusion, shame, and fear since those early days in Kanata when children's cruel taunts labeled me before I had any understanding of what those labels meant. The military's hypermasculine culture had only compounded this confusion, reinforcing the message that certain aspects of myself were unacceptable, dangerous even. "Don't Ask, Don't Tell" might have been officially repealed, but its shadow lingered in the minds and behaviors of those who found comfort in rigid definitions of identity.

Therapy became the laboratory where I gradually dismantled these internalized prejudices. Over countless sessions, I explored the complex terrain of my bisexuality—not through the distorted lens of others' stereotypes or expectations, but as my authentic experience. I uncovered the ways I had denied this part of myself, how I had engaged in relationships with both men and women while keeping emotional walls firmly in place, how I had treated my sexuality as something to be controlled rather than embraced. Detaching my self-worth from others' reactions proved to be one of the most challenging aspects of this journey. From childhood through my military career, I had internalized the message that something about me was fundamentally wrong, that the very essence of who I was invited rejection and ridicule.

Unlearning this conditioning meant questioning beliefs so deeply embedded in my psyche that they had become indistinguishable from the truth.

Gradually, painfully, I came to recognize that the very qualities that had made me a target were actually sources of strength. My sensitivity, once mocked as weakness, allowed me to connect deeply with others' pain. My empathy, derided as feminine, enabled me to understand perspectives beyond my own. My thoughtfulness, dismissed as overthinking, gave me insight into complexities others missed. Even my long eyelashes—a feature that had prompted jeers about looking like a girl—were simply a genetic trait, neither good nor bad, just uniquely mine.

The bullies who had targeted me throughout my life couldn't have known that they were inadvertently highlighting the very qualities that would. Eventually, allow me to heal, not just myself, but potentially others through sharing my story. The irony wasn't lost on me: what they had intended as weapons became the foundation of my resilience.

My love for animals, a constant thread through even my darkest moments, continued to provide both purpose and healing. I maintained my volunteer work at the animal shelter, finding profound connection with creatures who had experienced abandonment and mistreatment yet remained capable of trust and affection. The dream of one day creating a sanctuary for abandoned animals took shape in my mind—not just as a retirement plan, but as an extension of the healing journey I'd undertaken.

I witnessed the transformative power of unconditional love each time I worked with animals that had been neglected or abused. Their capacity to move beyond trauma, to embrace joy despite painful histories, offered a template for my own healing. My three cats have demonstrated this daily—Widget with his three-legged dignity, Carina with her playful curiosity, and Selene with her aloof confidence hiding the vulnerability she shared with those who gained her trust. They lived fully in the present, neither dwelling on past injuries nor anxiously anticipating future ones.

The decision to write this memoir emerged from a growing recognition that my story, though uniquely mine in its specifics, held universal elements that might resonate with others struggling to find authenticity amid expectation, to heal from wounds both visible and hidden. The process of translating lived experience into narrative forced me to examine my life from new angles and to find meaning in events that had once seemed merely painful or confusing.

Writing became another form of therapy, another way to integrate the disparate pieces of myself into a coherent whole. As I revisited the key moments that had shaped me from childhood. bullying to military betrayal to the gradual path toward healing—I gained perspective on how these experiences had contributed to the person I was becoming. The narrative wasn't complete, would never be complete as long as I continued to grow and evolve, but the act of telling it helped me recognize the trajectory from brokenness to something approaching wholeness.

Mindfulness remained a cornerstone of my daily practice, a way of anchoring myself in the present rather than being pulled into ruminations about the past or anxieties about the future. Through consistent meditation, I developed greater capacity to observe my thoughts without being dominated by them, to recognize when old patterns were asserting themselves, to choose responses rather than react from conditioning.

The concept of thriving took on new meaning as I progressed in my healing journey. Rather than a fixed destination I would one day reach, I came to understand it as a daily practice of showing up authentically, of making choices aligned with my values rather than my fears, of extending compassion to myself and others even when—especially when—it was difficult. Some days I managed this better than others, but the commitment to the practice remained constant.

Making amends became an important aspect of this journey—not just with others I may have hurt during my own periods of lashing out from pain, but with myself. I had to forgive the young man who had turned to alcohol and casual sex to numb unbearable feelings, who had built walls so high they kept out potential connection along with potential hurt, who had sometimes treated his own body and mind with less care than they deserved. This self-forgiveness didn't erase the consequences of those choices, but it did reframe them as understandable responses to extraordinary circumstances.

The scars I carried—both literal and metaphorical—gradually transformed from sources of shame into symbols of survival. They formed a roadmap of all I had endured and overcome, a testament to resilience rather than failure. The childhood trauma, the military betrayal, the years of struggling with identity and purpose—none of these defined me, but all of them had shaped me in ways I could now begin to appreciate.

My work helping agency employees connect with mental health resources took on deeper significance as I continued my own healing journey. Though I maintained professional boundaries and didn't share the details of my personal struggles, the empathy informing my work came from lived experience. Each time I helped someone take that first step toward getting support, I remembered my own terror and resistance, my own eventual relief at finding a path forward.

The themes that had followed me throughout life—isolation and connection, authenticity and pretense, running and standing still—continued to evolve as I integrated more fully the lessons of my past. I still experienced moments of doubt, days when old thought patterns reasserted themselves, times when the weight of accumulated trauma felt overwhelming. The difference was that I now had tools to navigate these challenges, a community of support to lean on, and a growing trust in my own capacity for healing.

Sharing my unfinished story became an act of faith—faith that vulnerability could be strength, that personal narrative could forge connection, that hope could exist in even the darkest corners of human experience. I had no illusions about the complexity of healing or the ongoing nature of the work, but I had come to believe in the possibility of transformation, in the human capacity to grow beyond limitation and expectation.

The past would always be part of me—its events aside. But my relationship to that past had fundamentally shifted. What once felt like a prison had become context; what once seemed like destiny had been revealed as merely prologue. The future remained unwritten, full of possibilities I was only beginning to recognize.

As the morning light shifted, casting new patterns across my desk, I thought about the young boy in Kanata who had felt so alone, so misunderstood, so different. If I could send a message back through time, I would tell him that the very qualities that made him a target would one day become his greatest strengths. That the sensitivity others mocked would develop into profound empathy. That the long eyelashes that invited ridicule were just one small part of a unique being worthy of acceptance and love.

I couldn't change that boy's journey—the isolation he would endure, the betrayals he would face, the years he would spend running from his own truth. But I could honor him by living authentically now, by embracing all the aspects of myself I had once tried to hide or change, by recognizing that the path to healing lay not in escaping the past but in integrating it into a more complex, more compassionate understanding of myself and the world.

Outside my window, a cardinal landed on the branch of a maple tree, its brilliant red plumage vivid against the backdrop of green leaves and blue sky. For a moment, I simply observed its presence—no analyzing, no projecting, just witnessing the beauty of a wild creature being exactly what it was meant to be. The bird had no concept of conforming or hiding; it simply expressed its nature through every aspect of its being.

In that moment of quiet observation, I felt a profound sense of connection—not just to the cardinal, but to all living things struggling and thriving in their own ways. The path forward wasn't about becoming someone new, but to all living things struggling and thriving in their own ways. The Path forward wasn't about becoming someone new, but about fully inhaniting the person I had always been beneath the layers of adaptation and self protection. It was about embracing authenticity not as a destination but as a practice, a daily choice to stand in my truth even when that truth defied easy categorization or external expectation.

The journey wasn't over; perhaps it never would be. But for perhaps the first time in my life, I wasn't looking for an exit, wasn't scanning the horizon for a place to hide. I was simply here, now, present to whatever might come next—imperfect, unfinished, authentic, alive.

Unspoken Truth Reflections:

1. What part of my childhood story have I never fully acknowledged; even to myself? *(This could be fear, instability, bullying, loneliness, or something I witnessed but didn't understand at the time.)*

____

____

____

____

2. Where did I learn to hide my feelings or silence my needs? *(Was it at home? At school? Around certain people?)*

____

____

____

____

3. How have those unspoken childhood truths followed me into adulthood? *(In relationships, confidence, boundaries, self-worth?)*

____

____

____

____

Trust in the Lord with your heart and lean not on your own understanding; in all your ways submit to him.

-Proverbs 3:5-6

Unspoken Battles Journal:

ACKNOWLEDGEMENTS

A special thanks to my literary team, Philip Hatterman and Daniel Gomez, my publisher, and Stefanie Trevino, DGE Publishing specialist. There was a lot of pain and darkness throughout my life, but this book has helped me tremendously... Thank you both for your support!

Also, a special thanks to my paternal and maternal grandparents. I'm grateful that you were my grandparents. I miss and love you all.

Finally, special thanks to my aunt Lillian for helping my mom raise me and being that solid rock and foundation!

To my grandparents, Mimi & Grandpa & Grandma Mary, whose love, strength, wisdom, and quiet sacrifices helped shape the person I became/becoming, this book is dedicated to you with love and gratitude.

In loving memory of my mother, whose love, strength, and presence continue to guide me every day.

IN LOVING MEMORY OF MY MOTHER

†

MARTHA ANN

I would like to thank a very, very special person in my life, my mom! Thank you for your unconditional love and unwavering support. You are my best friend forever and always. I love and miss you.

Your Mother
Is Always With You.

She's the whisper of the leaves as you walk
down the street, she's the smell of certain foods
you remember, flowers you pick,
the fragrance of life itself. She's the cool hand
on your brow when you're not feeling well,
she's your breath in the air on
a cold winter's day. She is the sound of
the rain that lulls you to sleep,
the colors of a rainbow. Christmas morning.

Your mother lives inside your laughter.
She's the place you came from,
your first home,
and she's the map you follow
with every step you take.
She's your first love, your first
friend, even your first enemy,
but nothing on Earth can separate you.
Not time, not space...
not even death.

RESOURCES

———†———

You are never alone, and help is always available. Your story is still being written; make sure you're the one holding the pen. The end of a personal relationship. The loss of a job. Everybody faces difficult times in life, and people cope with stressful situations in different ways. If you or someone you know is struggling, there are people who care and want to help. Whether you are at a crisis point or you are just ready to talk, please reach out. You are worth it.

National Suicide Prevention Lifeline: 988 is available 24/7. Crisis

Text Line: Text HOME to 741741 for free, 24/7 support

StopBullying.gov

National Alliance on Mental Illness (NAMI) **offers** support for mental health struggles at NAMI.org.

The Trevor Project (LGBTQ+ youth support): thetrevorproject.org or call 1-866-488-7386 or text START to 678678.

Confidential Crisis Support for Veterans and Their Loved Ones is available 24/7.

Veterans Crisis Line is available 24/7. You don't have to be enrolled in VA benefits or health care to connect with caring, qualified responders:

Call 988 and press 1. Chat at **VeteransCrisisLine.net/chat** or text (**838255**).

ABOUT THE AUTHOR

Cornelius Garnett is a retired Army veteran, government contractor, and survivor of the silent battles many never see. In Unspoken Battles, he shares a deeply personal journey through childhood bullying, toxic leadership, military life, emotional trauma, and the lasting effects of PTSD. With honesty and resilience, Cornelius opens the door to the struggles veterans and everyday people often carry in silence — anxiety, isolation, loyalty, heartbreak, and the fight to reclaim peace after years of conflict both inside and outside the uniform.

More than a story about pain, Unspoken Battles is about endurance, self-discovery, and overcoming obstacles without losing compassion or purpose. Through military service, personal setbacks, and rebuilding his life, Cornelius offers readers a raw and relatable look at what it means to survive, heal, and keep moving forward when life tests you the hardest.

Made in the USA
Monee, IL
16 September 2026

63296748R00056